WORKING WITH EXCLUDED GROUPS

Guidance on good practice for providers and

policy-makers in working with groups

under-represented in adult learning

**Based on the Oxfordshire
Widening Participation project**

Veronica McGivney

Dumfries
& Galloway
COUNCIL

niace
promoting adult learning

Widening Participation
The Oxfordshire
Strategic Partnership

Published by the National Institute of
Adult Continuing Education (England and Wales)

21 De Montfort Street
Leicester
LE1 7GE

NIACE has a broad remit to promote lifelong learning opportunities
for adults. NIACE works to develop increased participation in
education and training, particularly for those who do not have easy
access because of barriers of class, gender, age, race, language and
culture, learning difficulties and disabilities, or insufficient financial
resources.

The NIACE website on the Internet is http://www.niace.org.uk

Cataloguing in Publication Data
A CIP record of this title is available from the British Library

ISBN 1 86201 081 1

Contents

The groups least represented in education and training provision are those who are also the most socially and economically disadvantaged: long-term unemployed people; low-waged manual workers; people with poor literacy and no qualifications; members of some Black and Asian communities; older adults; homeless people; lone parents; full-time carers of sick or elderly relatives; ex-offenders; people with disabilities or learning difficulties; people on low incomes in rural areas or peripheral estates. Although educational opportunities and services may be available in the areas where they live, many members of these groups are either unaware of them or lack the confidence, time or material resources to take advantage of them. Others perceive learning as formal and irrelevant and something that other groups and social classes do.

Encouraging these groups to engage in education is not simple or straightforward. Widening participation is a complex and multi-faceted process which involves a range of inter-dependent elements: development work in the community (networking, contacting, consulting, negotiating); curriculum development (responding in a creative and flexible way to expressed interests and needs); student support (recognising barriers; using appropriate delivery and teaching/learning methods; providing both practical and learning support); provision of continuation strategies (guidance and progression pathways).

The following guidelines are based on the work of the Oxfordshire Strategic Partnership but also take into account other widening participation initiatives that have been conducted throughout the country.

The Oxfordshire Strategic Partnership was formed in the summer of 1997 in response to the invitation from the Further Education Funding Council to bid for funding to run innovative learning programmes with non-participating adults. The Partnership consisted of all the public sector further, higher and adult education providers in the County, two voluntary institutions, the LEA, the Heart of England Training and Enterprise Council, and the Employment and Careers services.

The Oxfordshire bid was accepted by the FEFC and the Partnership formed the Steering Group directing the project.

The project, which finished in June 1999, consisted of three main elements. Firstly, five action-research projects were commissioned to explore ways of reaching groups which existing data suggested were under-represented among learners. This provided a base of **experience** to inform the development of approaches to non-participating adults by providers in the County generally as well as by the local planning partnerships.

Secondly, a database of quantitative information was created to give an understanding of current patterns of participation in the County, and, by reference to overall population data, identify areas of particular under-representation. This provided a base of **information** to guide planning.

Finally, the Oxfordshire project established five local planning partnerships based on the five District Council areas in Oxfordshire with the responsibility of developing plans for widening participation in their areas. In producing plans, the partnerships drew extensively on the experience and information derived from the other project activities.

The five-action research projects form the basis of this guidance document. They sought to widen participation among specific target groups – low-qualified care workers, people in bail hostels and on probation; Asian men; workers and residents in isolated rural areas; and homeless young people.

In Banbury, a group of disaffected Asian secondary school students were involved in researching the experiences and attitudes towards learning amongst older Asian men. They used video recordings of interviews and discussions. Technical support was provided by media studies students who helped to build bridges between the young Asian men and the college of FE. Many insights were gained as to the learning needs of Asian men and the barriers preventing them from taking part.

In Oxford, the college of further education led a project which helped homeless young people to organise a series of roadshows to promote a new housing project for homeless young people. It showed that these young people were motivated to learn once they saw the relevance of the project to them. It also showed how the college had to develop its role as a base for living and personal support as well as for learning.

In Shrivenham, support staff employed at the Royal Military College were targeted through their employer, Granada Defence Services. Each worker was offered a 15-minute interview about his or her learning needs. As a result, 12% of the workforce became involved in tailor-made courses, including IT and basic skills.

In Oxford, carers from residential homes, who often have very little opportunity for training, were offered a free specially designed OCN-accredited programme with activities that could be used with those they cared for, e.g. reminiscence work, aromatherapy, art and crafts. The carers gained in confidence and started to develop new ideas for their work with the elderly.

In Nettlebed, an outreach programme recruited a group of adults with no recent experience of adult education by setting up a computer course at the local primary school. The project underlined the value of outreach work and of keeping learning local. It also showed the magnetic power of IT facilities in attracting new learners.

In Oxford, a joint project was set up between Adult Education, the Probation Service, bail hostel staff and residents. A programme of informal learning was devised that included discussion, guidance, group work and apparently recreational activities. It showed that, with plenty of detailed planning, negotiated learning activities and skilled group work, motivation could be stimulated and maintained.

In a parallel project, the Basic Skills Service worked with the Probation Service in assessing the literacy and numeracy levels of new offenders in the county. It revealed that 89% of respondents were operating at a literacy level below the level of an 11-old child. 34% were at a level that would make it hard to find or keep a job. 21% were at a numeracy level that would also make it difficult to find or keep a job. It showed the enormous potential for developing literacy and numeracy work with offenders and ex-offenders.

Further details of the projects are given on pages 17-26. The projects confirmed a number of established elements of good practice in widening participation and demonstrated some transferable 'principles of engagement' with the groups least represented in education and training.

1 Partnerships

Experience indicates that a multi-agency approach to widening participation among socially excluded groups is better than isolated and duplicated initiatives. There is an economic logic to sharing resources and expertise and it also helps the target groups (for example, if there is a plethora of different agencies helping the homeless without collaboration or co-ordination, this can lead to waste and confusion).

All the Oxfordshire projects worked with a number of partners. In working with homeless young people, for example, Oxford College of Further Education worked in collaboration with the Junction partnership and the Bridge (emergency accommodation) project; in targetting Asian men, Banbury Community Education Council worked with Banbury School and North Oxfordshire College; in working with offenders on probation and people in bail hostels, Cowley Community Education Council worked in collaboration with the City Youth Team, the New Start Adult Guidance Service and the Oxfordshire and Buckinghamshire Probation Service. Each of these had a named key worker to liaise on the project, as well as assistant wardens at two bail hostels. The rural isolation project involved Abingdon and Henley Colleges working with their local community education centres, particularly Faringdon and Chiltern Edge, as well as the LEA's basic skills service. Finally, the project dealing with people in low-skilled jobs was led by Headington Community Education Centre working with Oxford College and the WEA.

Collaboration was an intrinsic part of the Oxfordshire action-research projects, and the wider range of skills and resources that this approach put at the disposal of the project teams was a contributory factor to their success.

Collaboration in widening participation requires:

- Partnership between the voluntary and the statutory sector
- Prior agreement on goals, allocation of resources, deployment of staff and ways of operating
- Named contacts in each partner for liaison purposes
- Parity of status and respect for all partners
- Regular meetings, both formal and informal
- Representation in partnerships of the target group(s) and opportunities for them to participate in decision-making
- Continuity of commitment on the part of all partners
- A shared purpose.

Partnership initiatives in widening participation, such as those conducted in Oxfordshire, enable providers to explore jointly the kind of approaches that are effective with different groups and draw out common issues and lessons that will inform other lifelong learning initiatives aimed at people who are not habitual learners.

2   Reaching people

The results of house-to-house leafleting or door-knocking seldom justify the time and effort expended. Collective approaches are often more successful than individual approaches for several reasons. Engaging in education or training is not a habitual activity within some social groups, and many people are reluctant to be out of step with their communities by going against cultural norms. It is also easier to embark on something new and potentially intimidating as a group than as an individual. The success of workplace education development schemes can be partly attributed to the fact that all workers, irrespective of grade or status, have an entitlement and can participate alongside their work-mates without fear of stigma or ridicule.

3   Defining the target group

Widening participation requires a 'segmentation' approach with recruitment, curriculum and delivery methods specifically tailored to the characteristics, circumstances, priorities and norms of a group or community. The first task therefore is to define and locate the target group and identify their characteristics, barriers and needs.

Target groups should not be too broad. To give two examples: 'unemployed men' as a category can include people who differ widely in age, experience, educational and occupational background. Their interests and aspirations may be correspondingly diverse and what will appeal to one cohort will not necessarily appeal to another.

'Young adults outside of employment, education or training' may also be too broad a category. Action research conducted with this group found distinct differences in aspiration and attitude between those aged 16-18 and those aged 18 and over:

> *'The younger cohort was more interested in getting a job that would bring in enough money to satisfy their social requirements. The older cohort was more concerned about their longer-term prospects and needed income to support their more basic needs of food, shelter and clothing'* (Merton, B. 1999, 'Finding the Missing', *Adults Learning* Volume 10, Number 5).

Where possible, therefore, target groups need to be broken down into small and clearly defined categories. All the Oxfordshire projects focused closely on a distinct segment of the community. The rural project had the broadest target group. It worked with two separate rural communities: low-qualified manual workers in one of the largest local employers – the Royal Military College at Shrivenham – and residents of a small village (Nettlebed).

4   Development work

Simply transplanting existing provision from an education institution or centre to an outreach location will not necessarily widen participation. Nor will distribution of conventional publicity materials. Although such strategies may attract some new learners these may not include many members of the groups that are hardest for education agencies to reach. People who do not habitually engage in organised education and training tend not to respond to publicity unless this is again very clearly targeted. For example, enclosing messages with individual wage slips (as in the Royal College of Military Science in Shrivenham) or with Giro cheques (used to publicise the Learning Helpline during Adult Learners' Week) has proved effective in getting information to low-waged workers and unemployed people. In most cases, however, a proactive, one-to-one approach is the most successful strategy to employ with the groups that are the most difficult to reach. The nature of such an approach, however, needs to be carefully prepared.

The right staff

First, you have to have to appoint the right development or outreach workers. New groups are more easily drawn into education when they are contacted by people with characteristics and backgrounds similar to their own. People of the same gender or ethnic group, who speak the same language or have the same accent, and who have established local credibility, are far more likely to be accepted and trusted than those who do not have characteristics in common with the groups they are trying to work with. The Oxfordshire project working with Asian men would probably not have succeeded had it not had an Asian project worker.

The right skills

As well as the right characteristics development workers should have the right mix of skills. These include: good listening and communication skills; organisation skills; the ability to deal with a range of individuals and organisations at all levels; the ability to develop and maintain arrangements in diverse locations; and the ability to recognise and utilise local services and resources.

5   Networking

To reach different groups in the community involves considerable networking and negotiating with other agencies. In widening participation you are rarely dealing with a single target group since you also need to secure the co-operation of the agencies and key individuals in closest contact with that group. Development workers may need to work with several 'layers' of people before they can make direct contact with the people they are targeting. For example, ethnic minority adults have been reached by working first with younger people from the same community who have been contacted through local schools and community groups. This approach has proved effective in the Sheffield Black Literacy campaign and by Asian groups in Coventry. It was also used in the Oxfordshire partnership work. The approach is doubly effective as it targets both the older and younger cohorts.

Around the country, many low-qualified parents have been attracted onto family learning schemes and literacy workshops as a result of networking and collaboration with heads and teaching staff of local schools.

In Oxfordshire, academically under-achieving young Asian men in years 10-11 were identified through Banbury School. The group were trained both in producing videos and interviewing techniques. This gave them the expertise to conduct video- recorded interviews with older male relatives and key male members of the Asian community on their attitudes to education and educational interests. The interviews took place in community locations such as a mosque and workplaces.

Another effective strategy used in Oxfordshire has been to reach low-qualified workers through negotiation and collaboration with one of the largest employers in a rural area. This was the strategy used in the Shrivenham project.

Isolated populations are most effectively reached via local groups and organisations.

The outreach worker in the Nettlebed rural project in Oxfordshire net-worked with all the main local organisations: the local post office, health centre, a parent and toddler group, schools, pubs, the golf club, a care home and a young offenders' institute. The key link was with the local school where contact was made with the head teacher, staff, governors, caretaker, parents and children. Partnership with the school resulted in the organisation of computer courses for local people: *'the personal approach was absolutely vital and took time, effort and energy but this undoubtedly paid off. The helpful working relationship established with Nettlebed School was a factor in making students feel at ease and enabled them to make the best use of the course.'*

6   Negotiating with the gatekeepers

As these examples indicate, development workers succeed in reaching their target groups only after contacting and negotiating with other individuals – the *'gatekeepers'*. These may be community or religious leaders, head teachers, health visitors, employers, managers, bail hostel wardens, probation officers, wardens in hostels for the homeless, managers or wardens of day- or residential-care centres for the elderly, people with disabilities and people with learning difficulties etc. As found in the Oxfordshire projects, the gatekeepers have diverse characteristics, values, pressures and priorities and approaches to them need to be just as sensitive and responsive as approaches to the groups providers are trying to reach.

The Oxfordshire project targeted at low-qualified care workers started with identifying approximately 20 residential care homes. Owners and managers of these were sent an initial letter which explained the scheme and emphasised the value of raising worker education and skill levels. The letter invited managers to take part in 10-minute tele-phone interviews to assess the skill needs of the care homes and training needs of care workers. The letter was followed up by tele-phone contacts to arrange the interviews. Before these took place, employers were sent questionnaires to gather basic facts about the homes, their level of staffing and the training offered. After the interviews and when course details were finalised, employers were sent leaflets and covering letters inviting them to send 1-2 workers with no qualifications onto an OCN-accredited course:

'it turned out that frequent contact on the phone and in writing was essential for getting the message across. In some cases even this was insufficient and it seemed that a personal visit would have greatly increased my chance of success. I found that repeated contact enabled me to build a relationship with some of the employers even if only by telephone.'

Negotiating with the 'gatekeepers' is one of the most important – and sometimes most difficult – aspects of widening participation. Widening participation initiatives will not get off the ground unless they can be persuaded of their value. Although many individuals will be enthusiastic and helpful, gaining the co-operation of others may be a long and painstaking process requiring tact and persistence as workers found in the Oxford projects:

'Managers are key but they're overwhelmed with work and reorganisation. We didn't expect to have to persuade them. Some were not co-operative.'

'It was a lot of hard work asking for a simple process to be conducted.'

'Addressing groups of staff has proved time-consuming and arduous.'

Practical problems

In trying to work with the gatekeepers, development workers may encounter a number of practical problems. In some work environments such as care homes, prisons and bail hostels, there may be little continuity of staffing and frequent personnel changes. Staff may be under extreme and constant pressure. They may also be working on different shift systems and have little contact or communication with their colleagues. As a result, messages and information about any arrangements that have been set up may not be passed on. Thus development workers who have spent a considerable amount of time gaining the co-operation of one 'key' person may find they have to start the process of contacting, informing and persuading all over again with another. Dealing with the practical problems requires patience and persistence: repeated follow-up communications, preparatory meetings with as many relevant people as possible (relying on one can be a mistake) and frequent dissemination of information on the current stage of the project to all of them.

Attitudinal problems

Second, there may be *attitudinal* problems. Changing an organisational culture or the mindset of individuals can be far more difficult than persuading non-participants to participate. Efforts to contact particular groups can be seen as encroachments on individual territory and therefore resisted. Some people may be reluctant to co-operate because they do not perceive educational approaches as useful or necessary to the group in question. They may be over-protective towards the people in their charge or feel threatened by the idea of having better educated individuals working for or with them. As found in the Oxfordshire projects, some employers do not see the necessity of educating or skilling staff beyond the requirements of their particular job:

> *{They said} 'There's no need for this kind of thing.'*
> *'Although staff were keen, the manager wasn't.'*
> *'He doesn't see the necessity of skilling staff just for the sake of it.'*

Those who do co-operate in facilitating or setting up learning initiatives sometimes have a view of a group's learning interests and needs that is at variance with *actual* interests and needs, and which corresponds more with their own beliefs and attitudes. This can affect the kind of activities they are prepared to facilitate.

Messages about value

In order to deal with challenges such as these, development workers have to display considerable tact, persistence and persuasiveness. They need to enter into an early dialogue with community leaders and other gatekeepers about the nature and purposes of the educational activities proposed and their potential outcomes. Getting the messages right at this stage is crucial:

> *'Their {assistant wardens'} ownership and involvement with the aims of the project was of primary importance. As they have no formal background in education it was necessary for them to understand the educational significance of seemingly "recreational" activities and the value of listening to what people think.' (Oxfordshire project with residents of bail hostels)*

The value of working with gatekeeping individuals or organisations is not only that it is a means of reaching the target group; it is also a way of raising their own awareness of educational needs and the educational opportunities available.

Before anything meaningful can be set up, therefore, you need to win the hearts and minds of community gatekeepers. In order to give their support, they will need to feel a sense of ownership and commitment to an initiative. This means they must be persuaded of its value not only to the target group but also to themselves. Initial discussions need to make clear that they have more to gain than to lose (for example, workers might improve their work performance; become better team workers; become better at taking initiatives etc.).

Staff from the Oxfordshire Adult Basic Skills Service worked with Oxfordshire and Buckinghamshire Probation Service in conducting a screening test to assess the literacy and numeracy levels of all new Oxfordshire offenders. 85 offenders took part in the process which revealed that 89 per cent of them were operating at or below the literacy level of an 11-year-old child. This alerted probation officers to the scale of the problem and the Basic Skills Service have since been in discussion with the probation service about future basic skills provision for probation clients.

It should be noted that the gatekeepers themselves may have barriers that need to be addressed. Employers may be worried about staff shortages and the costs of releasing workers for education and training. Providers may therefore have to offer them some form of support in exchange for co-operation. In one of the Oxfordshire projects, owner/managers of care homes were offered a small sum to help provide cover for absent workers. In a similar scheme elsewhere, work experience arrangements were negotiated with participating employers so that the workers released for training were replaced by students who were at an advanced stage of the course.

7 Consulting the target group

It is only when the essential ground work has been conducted with the gatekeepers that one can start a dialogue with the actual target groups. The next key stage in widening participation is direct consultation with groups on their learning interests and perceived needs.

> In one of the Oxfordshire rural projects, contact with low-qualified workers in the Royal Military College was achieved with the co-operation of a manager of *Granada Services* who allowed leaflets to be attached to their weekly wage packets. The leaflets invited workers to attend a free and confidential 15-minute interview on their learning needs and stressed that learning would be accessible, responsive to needs and could help to change lives.15 people responded, followed by a further eight. *'The most important factor in establishing need was face-to-face information and guidance rather than on paper.'*

Cultural sensitivity

Communicating with groups who do not habitually engage in learning demands cultural sensitivity. Widening participation has to start from an informed understanding of group characteristics, circumstances, values and priorities. Some groups (Muslim Asians for example) have strong religious beliefs and cultural norms and well-meaning attempts to draw them into education will fail if they are not founded on a knowledge and understanding of these.

Different groups may have problems that make participating in organised learning activities difficult and these also need to be addressed at the planning stage. Many of the barriers are well known. For example:

- Low-paid, unqualified workers, especially those who work on a part-time or casual basis, often have considerable work and domestic pressures. They may work on different shifts which makes commitment to a regular learning session difficult. Manual workers are offered the least training by employers and often suffer from lack of confidence and low aspirations;

- Male manual workers often live from day to day, moving from casual job to casual job. This makes commitment to a learning programme difficult;

- Unemployed groups are often more concerned with finding jobs than entering education, and their readiness to participate in education can be hampered by fear of putting benefit payments in jeopardy;

- Rural residents and those living on large estates on the edges of towns often suffer from lack of transport facilities, poor local amenities and a dearth of accessible learning opportunities;

- Women with young children often have difficulties finding time to learn and accessing affordable childcare;

- Homeless individuals have multiple problems that inhibit attendance on learning programmes: lack of material resources, a transient lifestyle, vulnerability to crime, ill health and substance abuse;

- Members of ethnic minority communities may be deterred by inter-related family, cultural and religious pressures; low or stereotyped expectations; experiences of racism; lack of role models; language barriers; and a perception that western education has little of value to offer them;

- People with disabilities may be unable to participate because of lack of special access arrangements and support;

- Ex-offenders' readiness to participate may be affected by peer group pressure, lack of self-esteem and the greater priority of finding a job and an income.

Despite their diversity, many non-participating groups have problems in common, notably practical problems relating to low incomes and cultural barriers relating to group norms and prior experiences of education. It is well established that many adults are suspicious of any form of education because of failure to achieve at school. Recruitment approaches need to take into account how nervous and inadequate many people feel in relation to learning, which is why the language used in initial contacts and publicity is crucially important.

Conveying the right messages

Success or failure in widening participation often depends on the way in which initiatives are presented. To quote a comment made by one of the Oxfordshire project workers: *'Education needs to be packaged in a form that is acceptable to them'*. Sometimes this means using non-educational activities as a 'hook'. A community education worker on a deprived estate in Leicestershire suggests that in order to attract groups who are put off by the idea of education you need first: *'to provide anything that's **not** education: information and advice and support on things that concern local people. Back off on the educational sell!'*.

> A working men's club in Langold, a former mining area in Nottinghamshire, houses a resource centre that provides local people with information and advice on a range of matters such as local job vacancies and welfare benefits. The centre also provides informal learning activities in response to interests and needs and it has been found that people who visit for one thing (information on welfare benefits) often stay for another (social contacts; learning to use computers; courses in first aid). For many people without qualifications this has proved the beginning of a sustained learning pathway.

In their first contacts with non-participant groups, development workers have to be extremely careful in their choice of terminology, avoiding words which have negative connotations ('assessment', 'exams', academic jargon) and any terms or descriptions which imply that individuals have deficits that need to be remedied. Any proposed activities should focus on strengths not deficits.

In approaches to some groups (for example, young men, ex-offenders) it can be more effective to talk about *activities* rather than 'education' or 'learning', and to stress the potential short-term rather than long-term gains. With these and other groups that have a strong peer group culture, it can be a useful strategy to identify the opinion leaders – those whom others respect and are influenced by – and gain their co-operation. If they are enthusiastic and prepared to participate, others will follow.

8   Responding to identified interests, motivations and needs

Consultation with groups on the nature of the activities to be undertaken has to be genuine not tokenistic. It is very important for people who are disadvantaged educationally, socially and economically to know that their views and preferences are listened to and respected. A key point to remember is that our 'professional' view of what people want and need does not necessarily reflect what *they* feel they want and need. You cannot pre-define learning needs. To state the obvious, people will only engage voluntarily in learning activities if these are what they want and if they are seen to be relevant to them at their current life stage. Putting on existing courses in an outreach venue is not sufficient to engage the real non-participants. As a community education worker in Leicestershire has found: *'If we just put out a course programme and waited for people to come through the door, no-one would come.'*

Programme content

People working with new learner groups have found that the actual subject or focus of an initial learning programme is immaterial so long as it has been negotiated with, and is of interest and relevance to, the group concerned. Allowing groups to express their interests and participate in decisions about the kinds of activities that are organised for them encourages them to set their own learning agenda and gives them a sense of ownership which produces commitment to a programme. This was fully recognised in the Oxfordshire Partnership projects: the rural projects responded to an expressed interest in learning to use computers; the project with young Asian men responded to their preference for hands-on activities and interest in videos; the initiative with homeless young people consulted them on their ideas and suggestions for the new Foyer.

> In the Oxfordshire project with the homeless, a group of young people involved in a homeless project were invited to become involved in the consultation process for designing the city Foyer scheme. A series of workshops were held to identify what they wanted from the project. The workshops gave participants the opportunity to meet other young people as well as interested adults, and also showed them that their opinions were being taken into account.
>
> The workshops led to the idea of a roadshow and making a video about the project. A 22-week project was subsequently mounted by Oxford College of Further Education with the aim of producing a video as a centrepiece to the roadshow. This allowed the young people to acquire a range of new skills (editing, music skills, team-working, planning, evaluating).
>
> The most important thing was that the whole project was: *'completely driven by them'*. Some of the group have since enquired about other courses at the college.

Capitalising on motivations

Capitalising on dominant motivations is an effective strategy for bringing people into learning. Parents who have previously shown little interest in education can often be recruited to family literacy schemes when their children start school because they are strongly motivated to help their children learn and achieve. Young men are more likely to participate in learning if the programmes provided are unlike school and involve practical hands-on activities that build on their dominant interests such as music, sports, motor vehicles, computers etc.

In the Oxfordshire project working with young Asian men, the focus on video proved to be a very effective approach with that particular target group as there is a strong interest in videos in the Asian community.

According to the evaluation of the project: *'Making a video is a hands-on activity which produces immediate results. The resulting product enables young people to reflect on and evaluate their progress; to compare it with earlier attempts and to see the progress made. The ability to keep repeating a shot until it is right develops a desire to achieve good results. The process of editing, recording and researching was of great value'.*

Participants derived a number of important benefits from the project. These included: team-work skills, communication skills, problem-solving skills, technical skills, skills in the use and dissemination of information, interview design, survey skills and presentation skills. Recognising these skills led to significant increases in self-confidence and self-esteem. Participants received a Youth Award Certificate (bronze or silver) and an in-house certificate. This also boosted confidence: 'Attendance was virtually 100%. Participants were keen to continue video work after the project and initiated their own project, making a video of the local area to show the Council. They have got their friends and peer group involved and enthused.'

The scheme has also had a significant impact on the boys' performance and behaviour at school.

Keeping up the momentum

Having interested people in learning activities it is important to deliver these as soon as possible – while people are all 'fired up' – otherwise momentum, enthusiasm and confidence may wane. *'There's no point in recruiting people in May if there isn't going to be anything they can join till September.'*

New learners are often extremely nervous and it is important to keep in contact with them right up to the time of the course or programme designed for them:

In the Oxfordshire Nettlebed project, all students were contacted by telephone and letter on at least three occasions before the computer course started. This allowed people to discuss their expectations, prior learning and experience, course content, details of the venue and practical arrangements. These prior contacts were also useful in allaying fears, building confidence and reassuring people about the content and relevance of the course.

Flexibility

It is important to have some flexibility within initial learning programmes in order to adapt to the changing interests and needs of learners. Where people start in learning is not always where they eventually want to go. Many people initially choose subjects that are comfortable or 'safe' (stereotypical male or female areas) or which they think they ought to know about (computers). Participation in these frequently gives them the confidence and motivation to branch out into other learning areas. Tutors working with new learners frequently find that, as their confidence grows, new interests develop, ideas change and aspirations are widened. One community educator has found that it is wise to have help with basic skills always available as new learners often realise that, in order to achieve a newly identified goal, they need to improve their reading and writing skills.

9 Delivery

The location of learning programmes is of crucial importance. Many people, especially those from low-income groups in disadvantaged areas, are extremely hesitant about leaving their familiar territory. Even a mile down the road may be out of reach not just because of lack of transport (though this is often a problem) but psychologically and culturally. It has been found in some areas that some jobless men do not move within a mile or so of their territorial 'comfort zone' in a 6-month period. Accessible local provision is therefore essential. A typical comment from a learner in the rural project in Oxfordshire was: *'I wouldn't have come if it hadn't been local'*.

The area in which provision is delivered must be one that is appropriate and congenial to the target group. In the Oxfordshire work with young Asian men, the East Street Centre was chosen as a venue because it is multicultural and in a multicultural district where the group feel comfortable.

Since one of the problems in rural areas is a lack of education centres and institutions, a way of providing local opportunities is to explore the possibility of opening up to the community the facilities and equipment in local enterprises or schools. In the Isle of Wight, for example, the best computer facilities are in local schools and these have now been made available for adult IT courses in after-school hours.

In some areas with scattered populations and spread-out residential estates, mobile education services regularly visit different sites offering information on education and work opportunities, help with basic education, IT training and other learning services. Some have upper decks with supervised crèches or play facilities. Examples are the Bolton Opportunities Bus, the Liverbus (part of the Liverpool community education service) and the Dove Valley Community Bus in South Derbyshire. Facilities such as these provide a valuable first step back into learning for many people who are unable or unwilling to travel further afield to make contact with potentially intimidating education institutions.

Learning venues

The venues used for learning should be as open, welcoming and informal as possible, and as far as possible, staffed by people who reflect the composition of the population. If the centres or premises used are seen as the preserve of a particular social or ethnic group or if they are dominated by one or other gender, they will not attract people who do not have those characteristics. One of the reasons frequently given for the paucity of male students in adult and community education is the fact that centres often appear to be staffed and frequented exclusively by women. A wider mix of staff (especially outreach development staff and tutors) would attract a wider mix of learners and have a valuable role model effect.

Flexibile arrangements

In widening participation it is often necessary to take risks and to be experimental and adaptable in meeting the needs of learners. This may mean allowing some flexibility within course timing and delivery. With groups such as residents of bail hostels and homeless people it is difficult to ensure regular attendance and keep to fixed timetables. Because of the uncertain and transient situation of these people, the composition of groups is likely to change from week to week. Similar problems have been encountered in work with young unemployed men, many of whom move in and out of the informal economy in order to make a living. With such groups continuity of attendance is unlikely and providing short taster courses or drop-in sessions may be the most effective response. For other groups such as women with caring commitments or shift workers, the timing of provision needs to be tailored to their specific circumstances. In Birmingham, for example, colleges have opened during weekends to offer low-qualified workers short TEC-supported training courses. This has proved a successful way of attracting people back into learning, and many have subsequently signed up for longer programmes.

With some ethnic minority groups, programme planning needs to take account of the timing of religious festivals.

Working with small numbers

It is inevitable (and sometimes desirable) when working with new learners that groups will initially be small as it takes time for trust and confidence to grow. However, it is commonly found that over time there can be an important 'ripple' effect. Once people see friends or family members learning and enjoying and benefiting from the process, they often want to follow their example. Nevertheless, one of the principal barriers to widening participation has, until recently, been the difficulty of obtaining funding for innovative work with small groups. A substantial part of post-16 funding has been tied to student numbers and outcomes with the result that development work in the community – something which is time- and staff-intensive with uncertain and unpredictable outcomes – has been difficult to support. New initiatives such as Widening Participating partnerships, the Adult and Community Learning Fund and lifelong learning plans, are enabling providers to be more flexible and innovative in their efforts to engage a wider cross-section of the population in learning.

10 Learner support

Practical support

The groups least represented in education and training are often those with fewest material resources. For many people even a small fee can be a deterrent, especially if they already perceive education as something inaccessible and relevant only to other social groups and classes. Provision of some free or low cost, short courses is a well-established means of attracting people back into learning. Groups on very low incomes or in difficult circumstances, such as homeless people, should also be helped with travel costs and where possible offered meals or refreshments. In the Oxfordshire project with homeless young people, participants received both a travel allowance and meals.

> Basic skills workers targeting 'disaffected' young people in Wales have found that provision of meals and small financial rewards for achievements is an effective way of attracting that group to provision that they rapidly come to value and enjoy for its own sake.

There is a range of other types of support that learners may require:

- Provision of childcare facilities or help with the costs of childcare is an extremely important support for parents. Without this many women with few or no qualifications would be unable to return to learning.

- Special access arrangements (and sometimes equipment) are necessary to enable people with disabilities and learning difficulties to participate in organised learning programmes.

- People living in isolated estates or rural areas may require support with travel costs and arrangements. Some further education colleges in rural areas organise buses that collect and return people at different times throughout the day.

- Some ethnic minority groups require attention to their cultural traditions (e.g. single-sex classes) and dietary patterns.

For new learners it is often the little things that are most important – a courteous and helpful response to a telephone enquiry; a building that is welcoming and well-lit; provision, before a course starts, of details about the exact location of venues and meeting rooms. Many people are so nervous about returning to education that tutors find they need to accompany them into the building at the time of a first session.

A community educator working on a deprived estate in the midlands reports that a bad initial experience in an education centre or institution – an impatient or unhelpful response from a receptionist for example – is rapidly transmitted along the bush telegraph and significantly puts back the cause of widening participation.

A good experience is just as rapidly transmitted. In the Oxfordshire Nettlebed project: *'as news of the success of the first {computer} course reached other people, a more diverse group of students enrolled'*.

Peer support

People are more readily persuaded to participate in education when they know that others from their peer group or local community are doing it. A number of projects throughout the country are currently training local people as animateurs, signposters or 'learning champions' to inform and advise others in their communities about learning opportunities. Often these are people who have themselves participated in learning activities and can testify to their value.

> **A project for homeless people in Walsall which offers accommodation, training and practical support, trains residents as peer mentors to befriend, motivate and support other young homeless people and act as positive role models.**

Learning support

Many new learners need learning support in the form of ongoing individual and group guidance, regular feedback and small group work. They may also require a small step approach to learning that recognises incremental achievements.

Some adult learners need to brush up their literacy and numeracy skills. Others need help with English as a second language or with study skills. If it is not possible to provide this kind of support within an initial learning programme, tutors should be able to direct individuals towards organisations or individuals who can provide these services.

Learning support can also be provided by the teaching and learning methods used. Many studies emphasise the need to design learning for non-traditional learners in such a way as to ensure early success and boost confidence. Learners' confidence can be raised by pacing course content so that there is a gradual increase in difficulty, and by using feedback from students to inform or change course design.

In widening participation, teaching and learning methods need to be tailored to group characteristics and preferences. Informality in approach, method and delivery is essential for putting people at their ease. The following quotation from the Oxfordshire project with under-achieving Asian boys illustrates how the methods used were particularly appropriate for this target group:

> 'The first session was magic. We kept a low profile and left it to the youth worker. He immediately got them doing it {using a video} and editing. So there was an instant result. With young people this is crucial. There was no paper. They started to learn straight away. It was immediate engagement. There was no lengthy discussion. We didn't talk too much at this stage about what we were hoping they would do. There was gradual immersion, bringing in things when we thought they were ready.'

Certification

Many people without qualifications welcome the opportunity to have their achievements recognised. However mentioning accreditation too early, before people's confidence has grown, can be intimidating and tutors find that, with some groups, it is best to introduce the idea very gradually. Employing a flexible, unit-based system such as Open College Network accreditation, which allows learners to reflect on their prior as well as current learning and build up a portfolio, has been found effective in starting people on the accreditation process and boosting their self-esteem.

The Oxfordshire partnership project with care workers held a pre-course meeting with participants. This helped them to reflect on their learning experiences, boosted their confidence and introduced them to the OCN credit. Workers were careful to ensure that the formal OCN paperwork was as unthreatening as possible. This gradual approach generated positive attitudes to the idea of accreditation.

---

11 Exit/Continuation Strategies

Widening participation initiatives should always include some form of exit strategy. Since many are short-term, they may raise expectations that may not be met. At the end of an initial learning programme, whatever its length, learners should not be left 'in the air'. They should be offered advice on how to continue learning or progress to something else. This might be done through incorporating information and guidance on other local learning opportunities at a later stage in the programme; helping learners to compile a portfolio that they can use to access other programmes or jobs; supplying them with a list of useful addresses and contacts or providing drop-in 'after care' support sessions. All of the Oxfordshire projects tried to offer learners continuation strategies. In the work with bail hostel residents, for example, learners were provided with a portfolio of contacts and shown how to develop different ways of presenting what they had done as an aid to gaining future employment.

If the initiative has been organised by a college or education centre, learners should be made aware of the other opportunities they provide and where possible, outreach provision should be articulated with other programmes offered by the same provider. Some tutors working with new learners have organised group visits to local colleges or made arrangements for providers to put on taster courses in the local venue. The enlisting of existing mature students as ambassadors or mentors has proved particularly effective in attracting people with similar characteristics into education centres and institutions that they would have otherwise avoided.

12 Embedding

Widening participation initiatives involving partnerships and special funding can achieve a great deal. Project workers throughout the country have reported positive changes in attitudes to learning both among the 'gatekeepers' and among target groups; as well as achievements that have had a positive impact on individuals, families and communities. However, this work needs to be embedded otherwise it will affect only a few individuals. Short-term projects are only short-term projects. However successful they are, they can only make minimal changes to the composition of the learning population.

Educational development workers, outreach workers (or whatever title one chooses to give them), are the real key to widening participation. Networking with different agencies and communicating with and listening to people on their own territory, involve a wider and more complex range of skills than those required for teaching people who voluntarily attend courses organised in a dedicated educational environment. The time, effort and energy required for development work in the community therefore needs to be recognised and supported. Too often development workers are appointed on a short-term or part-time basis and the potential impact of their work is consequently limited. If we wish to bring more groups into learning, development workers need to be appointed on a longer-term basis and have parity of status with institution-based staff.

To widen participation to any significant degree requires a consistent and long-term approach, sustained investment in development work in the community, and funding arrangements that enable flexibility and innovation in providing for new groups. Development work is costly in the short term but the long-term gains can be immense for individuals, families and communities. If participation can be widened among the groups most under-represented in the post-school education and training system, this would result in a significant change in public perceptions of education and significantly enhance efforts to create a culture of lifelong learning.

Perceptions will only change when education and training provision is seen to attract a greater cross-section of the public and when participating in education is seen as a normal, acceptable and beneficial everyday activity.

ANNEX

The Oxfordshire Widening Participation Project

Action-research projects

Oxfordshire Widening Participation Project

Action-research projects

This good practice guidance report is based extensively on the action-research element of the Oxfordshire project, and this annex gives further details of the work undertaken.

The project was one of 26 nationally approved by the Further Education Funding Council in September 1997 to explore ways of widening participation. The Oxfordshire scheme contained three main elements: a number of 'action-research' projects designed to increase experience of working with under-represented groups; a data collection and analysis element designed to increase information about current patterns of participation; and a planning element in which five local planning groups developed participation plans for their areas taking into account the experience and information gained through the other project elements.

Five target groups were identified and projects were set up to try to involve them in learning. Each project was run by a partnership of providers, in most cases involving the Adult Education Service, a further education college and at least one other agency.

The target groups were:

- Asian men
- Homeless young people
- Offenders and ex-offenders
- Carers within private sector residential care
- Isolated residents of rural areas.

More detailed information is given on the following pages and at the end there is a list of contacts for each project.

Cherwell action-research project – Asian men in Banbury

Main partners: Banbury Community Education Council, Banbury School, North Oxfordshire College.

Client groups: Under-achieving young Asian men in years 10 and 11 at school.
Older men in the same community.

Channels: Young men were recruited through their school.
Older men became involved through the school participants.
Use of project workers with links into the community.

Messages to client groups: Value of learning in coping with change in working life.
Learning can be a practically based activity with close relevance to the real world.

Purpose and methods:

To stimulate an interest in learning among under-achieving young people from an ethnic minority background; and at the same time to find out more about the needs of older members of the community.

These dual aims were realised through the project's approach through which the younger participants interviewed the older group members about their experiences and attitudes towards learning and recording the process on video.

Problems over communication:

There was initial distrust over the aims of the project and its method of video recording. This distrust was overcome by the project outreach workers; one a youth worker, the other a member of the Asian community herself, who had the credibility to reassure participants of the project's integrity.

Findings on learning and motivation:

The primary need in this community is to take up work and therefore post-16 learning is not always seen as a priority for young people.

Language and cultural barriers are still present within the educational system: the design of the curriculum, and learning materials, are not well oriented towards learners with this background.

Features of learning programmes:

Video/new technology medium;

Involvement of FE and HE media studies students;

Took place off school site;

Environment multicultural and supportive;

Alternative programme with clear learning outcomes.

Summary of learning points

- The target group was reached through a particular organisation (the school) which conveniently brought the group members together in a systematic fashion;

- School students were used as the entrée into the wider ethnic community in reaching the older community members who acted as the interviewees;

- The relevance for working and adult life of the project activities conveyed the right messages about the saliency of learning;

- The basis of the project in new technology was (a) interesting and relevant to the participants (b) suggestive of wider possibilities for learning and work (c) impressed the group of interviewees;

- The credibility of the project workers was key in defusing hostility and distrust;

- The use of informal learning methods and an environment outside school was essential in winning over disaffected and excluded groups;

- The links between FE, school, and community education were vital in enriching the project and made it more likely to result in learner progression;

- The project uncovered cultural issues which the providers don't currently fully address.

Shrivenham action–research project – Rural isolation (1)

Main partners:	Abingdon College, Faringdon Area Community Education, Vale Division outreach service, Oxfordshire LEA Basic Skills service.
Client group:	Non-participating adults with few qualifications in an isolated rural area. The group the project worked with were employed as support staff at the Royal Military College in Shrivenham by Granada Defence Services.
Channels:	Meetings were held with both organisations to obtain facilities and support for the project. Contact with the client group was made through leaflets, and messages in wage packets. The project worker was invited by Granada to approach potential learners in the workplace.
Messages to client groups:	Learning has the potential to change lives.
Purpose and methods:	To encourage participation by non-learners especially those requiring basic skills help. To convince employers of the value of systematic learning for their staff and for the efficiency of their organisation.
	Each worker was offered a 15-minute guidance interview with the prospect of suitable learning provision being made available particularly in basic skills. 12% of the workforce became involved in this way.
Findings on needs/ motivation:	Learners needed provision to be reliable, local and achievable. Face-to-face guidance and information a must. Provision needs to be tailor made with opportunities for progression, accreditation, development as autonomous learners.

Summary of learning points

- Target group was reached through the medium of an employer bringing together a large number of potential clients in one location;

- IT and basic skills were the key learning needs, along with confidence-building etc;

- It was essential to win the support of the employer in order to reach the client group;

- The problems of rural isolation and possible lack of transport were overcome by focusing the learning in the workplace at times convenient to the learners;

- There are possibilities for extending the work to the wider community using RMCS facilities;

- There is a need for sufficient development and needs-analysis time by the providers;

- There is a need for arrangements to maintain and embed the initiative beyond the pilot phase.

Nettlebed action-research project – Rural isolation (2)

Main partners:	Henley area community education centres, South Division outreach service, Henley College, Nettlebed School.
Client groups:	People with few qualifications and no recent history of learning living in a rurally isolated area (Nettlebed).
Channels:	Through local institutions especially the primary school; through visits to outlying areas; through posters and leaflets.
Messages to client groups:	Absolute beginners welcome; free course available.
Purpose and methods:	To find out about the learning needs of such a community; and how to overcome barriers to participation: by researching the local needs and making provision within the locality for a course of high demand (IT).
Problems over communication:	No particular problems: course quickly full and a second running.
Findings on needs/ motivation:	Particular requirement for this subject area. Learner enthusiasm where provision was local and accessible.
Features of learning programmes:	Short weekly programme held during the day in the school using computers lent by a neighbouring Community Education Centre.

Summary of learning points

- Recruitment of the school to be the local learning centre was central to the success of the initiative with possibilities for further development of the local learning centre concept;

- A large number of personal contacts were made through the use of an outreach worker;

- There was evident demand for this kind of provision;

- There is a case for a basic curriculum to be offered in a wide range of localities of which IT would be one component;

- There is consideration for wider provision of IT through mobile units;

- It was mainly non-participants who attended: men as well as women.

City action-research project – Choice for carers

Main partners:	Headington Community Education Centre, Oxford College of Further Education, the Workers' Educational Association.
Client groups:	People with few qualifications working in an occupational area (private sector residential care) with little prospect of further learning. Their employers.
Channels:	20 homes were identified, written to, issued with a questionnaire, telephoned; homes then leafleted. 11 applications were received from 7 homes.
Messages to client groups:	Learning has value in developing employees' confidence, creativity, and ability to acquire other skills.
Purpose and methods:	To encourage people with little opportunity for education and training at work back into learning. To convince employers of the value of learning for employees in less skilled and prestigious posts.
	Employees eligible for the programme were offered a specially designed OCN-accredited programme with course topics around reminiscence, aromatherapy, and art and craft; with increased confidence, personal development, and greater resourcefulness in dealing with their work as intended outcomes.
Problems over communication	Hostility among a small number of employers; general pressure and some times disruption in the homes which was unconducive to systematic learning; concept of learning leading to improved performance not always accepted by employers.
Findings in needs/motivation:	Learners gained increased confidence in dealing with their work and developed new ideas for working with elderly; they gained enjoyment; stimulation; were better motivated.

Summary of learning points

- Client groups were reached through an intensive programme of outreach work with employers;

- A continuous process of dialogue with home managers was essential for the approach to result in participation;

- There was a high success rate in attracting learners to the course;

- Much learning was found to be already in progress in some homes but not usually systematic or continuous;

- The programmes offered by the project were broad-ranging in content but effective in developing specific skills relevant to work;

- There were many problems over release of staff;

- The care workers who came on to the course were from homes where the care managers were already supportive of the idea of learning. In order to reach people working in homes which were less responsive, more outreach time would be necessary to allow for personal visits to build up relationships with home managers.

City action-research project – Homelessness

Main partners:	Oxford College of Further Education, the Bridge project, Oxford City Council.
Client group:	Homeless young people living in Oxford City and involved in City projects such as the Bridge, the Foyer scheme, and the Young Builders Self Build project.
Channels:	The lead partner was Oxford College of FE. Contact with the target group was made through their association with the above projects. The formal occasion for the contact was consultation work on the Junction Partnership initiative (development of centres and services for young people in Oxford funded through the City Single Regeneration Budget). Initial contact was established through a workshop for young people on how best to establish and promote the Junction concept.
Messages to client groups:	This project involved the young people in undertaking a complex programme of activity (organising a series of roadshows to promote the Junction) and once the value of the activity had been identified, it was easy for participants to accept a related programme of learning.
Purpose and methods	To find out about the learning needs of disaffected young people and to develop a relevant, satisfying and socially supportive curriculum. Young people were encouraged to take an active and creative role in the programme, and to undertake related learning activities.
Problems over communication:	The transient nature of the group and their sometimes *ad hoc* lifestyle and the degree of structure and formality required, were problems the project overcame.
Findings on needs/ motivation:	Group members: • have an interest in their achievements being recorded; • need the college as a base for living and support as well as learning; • are responsive to learning when the personal relevance is clear.
Features of learning programmes:	Highly flexible, informal, based on short concentrated units responding to the transience of the group members, but with a cumulative coherence for those who stay. The programme has a practical outcome in the form of roadshows, and part of the objective is to demonstrate the value of learning to other young people attending the events.

Summary of learning points	• Development of the college as a social and welfare as well as a learning centre was necessary for this group to function; • It was essential to use existing agencies in touch with the group; • The saliency of learning was demonstrated to the group through practical activities; • The participants themselves were key players in contacting and encouraging participation among other similar young people; • The project demonstrates that learning has an immediacy for even the most disaffected, when the environment and approach are right; • The structure of learning was suited to the needs of a transient group.

City action-research project – Offenders (1): Bail hostel residents

Main partners:	Cowley Community Education Council, New Start Adult Guidance Service, Oxford City Youth Team, Oxon and Bucks Probation Service.
Client groups:	People on bail awaiting the date of a court appearance/result of a court appearance. There is no statutory provision within the probation service for this group.
Channels:	Partnership approach involving Oxford City Community Education – youth, adult and new start adult guidance – the Oxfordshire and Buckinghamshire probation service, City bail hostel staff and residents.
Messages to client groups:	Practical value of learning (find way around a new town); personal (keep fit); curiosity; ownership of their own learning. Recognition of existing skills and experience. Respect for contributions and opinions. Active listening to residents/participants and obvious responses to points raised/interests voiced.
Purpose and methods:	To understand the developmental needs of people often with very low levels of prior attainment, and grievances and resentment against the system; and to stimulate their interest in learning through formal and informal methods including one-to-one discussion sessions, informal group work, much use of seemingly recreational activities as the basis for learning; continual need to reinforce the basic messages about learning.
Problems over communication:	Resentment on the part of participants because away from home, family; lack of continuity among residents and also assistant wardens; these problems were sometimes resolved through listening hard; importance of briefing outside providers on the issues.
Findings on needs/ motivation:	Residents open to suggestions about their future learning (a transitional time) but learners need to decide their programme of activities; wardens need to be genuinely supportive; a central member of the group needs to endorse the programme to give it credibility. Lots of standard psychological barriers to participation.
Features of learning programmes:	Highly tailored, individual attention, flexibility of design, listening and support basic skills and personal development, learning and life merging.

Summary of learning points

- There is a need for close communications between the partner organisations and understanding of each others' methods;

- There was development of understanding among the assistant wardens;

- There was a high degree of informality/flexibility;

- Participants' sense of ownership was paramount;

- Supporting/nurturing elements;

- Importance placed on listening to participants' views.

Action-research project – Offenders (2): Key skills screening in work with offenders

Purpose: To provide evidence about the literacy and numeracy levels of offenders on probation in Oxfordshire, both in order to establish what these are and in order better to assess what kinds of provision will be most effective in meeting offenders' needs.

Process: Staff from the Oxfordshire Adult Basic Skills Service in discussion with OBPS (Oxfordshire and Buckinghamshire Probation Service) drew up a screening test to assess the literacy and numeracy levels of all new Oxfordshire offenders, delivered by probation staff as part of the initial interview process which all new clients undergo.

Participants: Between September 1998 and February 1999, a total of 85 offenders from all parts of the county took part in the screening process.

Findings: **Literacy:**

- 89% of respondents were operating at level 1 or below, ie. at or below the level of an 11-year-old child;

- 34% were operating at a level (below level 1) which would make it difficult for them to find and keep a job, and a further 22.5% were operating at border-line entry level/ level 1 point;

- 6% were below entry level, ie. were practically unable to write anything at all.

Maths:

- 21% were operating at a level (below level 1) which would make it difficult for them to find and keep a job.

Achievements of the survey:

- The survey successfully introduced probation staff to the idea of basic skills screening for all new offenders – though more work needs to be done in this area;

- Confirmed the levels of poor literacy among Oxfordshire offenders;

- Will inform discussions with the Probation service about the future of basic skills provision for probation clients in the light of the service's new training and employment strategies.

Contacts for action research projects

Overall contacts for the Widening Participation project
Stephen Ashworth – Oxfordshire County Council – Macclesfield House, New Road, Oxford OX1 1NA. Tel: 01865 815358 : Fax: 01865 791637 E-mail: stephen.ashworth@oxfordshire.gov.uk

Bob Challis – Principal, Abingdon College, North Court Road, Abingdon, OX14 1NN. Tel: 01235 541042 : Fax: 01235 541019
E-mail: bchallis@abingdoncollege.ac.uk

Bail hostel residents
Carole Lushington – New Start Adult Guidance Team Co-ordinator – East Oxford Education Complex, Union Street, Oxford OX4 1JP.
Tel: 01865 798081

Key skills assessment of offenders
Vanessa Kenyon – ABS Unit – Oxford College of FE, Blackbird Leys Precinct, Cuddesdon Way, Oxford OX4 5HN.
Tel: 01865 778827 : E-mail: adultbsu@rmplc.co.uk

Homelessness project
Pam Woolley – Oxford College of Further Education, Oxpens Road, Oxford OX1 1SA. Tel: 01865 245871 : Fax:01865 248871:
E-mail: pam_woolley@oxfe.ac

Asian men in Banbury
Patricia Scott – Head of Community Education – Banbury Community Education Council, East Street Centre, East Street, Banbury, OX16 7LJ. Tel: 01295 266763 : Fax: 01295 266763 : E-mail: bancec@eclipse.co.uk

Rural isolation (1): Shrivenham
Angela Wood – Vale Divisional Access Co-ordinator – Community Education Office, Carswell School Annex, Conduit Road, Abingdon. OX14 1DB. Tel: 01235 537667 : Fax: 01235 537642

Steve Billcliffe – Abingdon College, Northcourt Road, Abingdon. OX14 1NN. Tel: 01235 541044 : Fax 01235 541019
E-mail: sbillcliffe@abingdoncollege.ac.uk

Rural isolation (2): Nettlebed
Sheila Bruce – Head of Community Education, Henley area – Chiltern Edge Community Education Centre, Reade's Lane, Sonning Common. RG4 9LN. Tel: 0118 9723362 : Fax: 0118 9721271
E-mail: cecec@eclipse.co.uk

Choice for carers
Alison Soskice – Head of Centre – Headington Area Community Education Centre, Northway Centre, Dora Carr Close, Headington, Oxford. OX3 9RU. Tel: 01865 768359 : Fax: 01865 741173